Rural Score
& other poems

by

Lina Belar

Finishing Line Press
Georgetown, Kentucky

Rural Score

Copyright © 2017 by Lina Belar
ISBN 978-1-63534-246-8 First Edition
All rights reserved under International and Pan-American Copyright Conventions. No part of this book may be reproduced in any manner whatsoever without written permission from the publisher, except in the case of brief quotations embodied in critical articles and reviews.

ACKNOWLEDGMENTS

At the Library—published as a Broadside by *Northern Lights Library Network*
Bells—published in *Lake Region Review* 2014
Winter Roulette—published in *Lake Region Review* 2013
Parade—published in *Talking Stick* 2014
Tornado—published in *Talking Stick* 2014
Signs of Fall—published in the *Perham Focus Fall Scene* magazine 2014

Publisher: Leah Maines

Editor: Christen Kincaid

Cover Art: Lina Belar

Author Photo: Don Hoffmann

Cover Design: Elizabeth Maines

Printed in the USA on acid-free paper.
Order online: www.finishinglinepress.com
        also available on amazon.com

Author inquiries and mail orders:
Finishing Line Press
P. O. Box 1626
Georgetown, Kentucky 40324
U. S. A.

Table of Contents

Free Ticket 1

Shy Girls 2

Before the Paris Shows 3

At the Library 4

On the Way to Duluth 5

Bells 6

Rural Score 7

At the Café during WeFest 8

Along the Northern Pacific Route—Economic Lesson #1 9

Washington, D.C.—Economic Lesson #2 10

Winter Roulette 11

February 12

Slow Melt 13

Fast Spring 14

Parade 15

Tornado 16

One Perfect Summer Evening 17

Late Summer 18

Signs of Fall 19

Home Again 20

For Jerome

Free Ticket

For a free ticket to anywhere
in the 48 contiguous United States,
Canada, Mexico, Puerto Rico and the Caribbean
I wait at the airport for three more hours
drink bad coffee, read trashy novels
and think, "This isn't so bad, I could
waste this much time watching TV,
washing clothes, or wearing out
cheap tennis shoes in a game of volley ball."

For a free ticket to anywhere
I have given up a seat on the noon flight
and gained the rest of the afternoon to find
a comfortable position on badly contoured seats
in a waiting room noisy with more impatient travelers.

Busy executives flash electronic devices,
children with imported tans play musical chairs.
Across from me, a beautiful girl
caresses the cheek of a slouching youth
in olive drab who scans the room as though
to reassure himself that no one is watching.

I'm glad for this delay since it postpones
the prospect of one more homecoming
without your smile to welcome me.
For a free ticket to anywhere
I've caused myself a little inconvenience
but in the end I've gained the illusion that
if I can go somewhere else,
you might be there, too.

Shy Girls

Shy girls
talk too loud in restaurants
stick their arms out straight
to shake the hands of everyone they meet,
think of all the things they should have said out loud
and cringe in shame remembering those they did.

Shy girls
wear too much make-up,
pick the trumpet to play
in 5th grade band
look for hidden meanings
in everything they hear.

Shy girls
think other girls are prettier,
smarter, luckier, but know
they have something
most girls can't match.

Shy girls
carry within their narrow chests
the soul of a turtle
slow, persistent, persevering.

Shy girls
outlast the rest.

Before the Paris Shows

The length of this year's skirt
was a subject of intense debate.
All winter, the women in my family
paged through Vogue magazines
sifting gossip from fashion houses for clues.

By the time spring season arrived, names like
Chanel, Dior, Givenchy, were daily household words.
Finally, the famous couturiers spoke.
This year, they decreed the hemline would be
a daring one inch above the knee.

Mannequins in department stores
complied at once, flaunted clothes
we could never afford to buy.
From our closets we gathered skirts
and dresses, filled our sewing baskets
with needle, thread and scissors.

All week long we picked, folded, measured,
basted and pressed the finished hems in place
at the exact right length.
We had such a desire to be fashionable.
But, despite all our work,
they were still last year's clothes.

At the Library

All summer long, my sister and I
read books that take us places we have
never been and will likely never see.

I am to the T's in the
adult fiction section of the Public Library,
a faded Victorian house filled with books
tended by two maiden women
who sort and clean donated books,
catalogue them, honoring Dewey.

I read everything by Erich Maria Remarque,
acquire a stunning grasp of the vernacular
I expect to keep well hidden.
My sister, two years younger,
reads books like "The Bobbsey Twins"
and Nancy Drew mysteries.

"Is that a good one," I ask her one day.
"Oh yes," she answers, "I'm almost done,
but there's another book in the series."
We both breathe sighs of relief knowing
there are still more worlds left to travel.

On the Way to Duluth

> "Not long ago, I was in northern Minnesota and I could not
> help but think what a contrast it is now to what it was fifty years
> ago and I wondered that man could destroy a world in so short
> a time when it took nature thousands of years to create it."
>   From *Memories* by E.H. Pelton
>   employed by the lumber company
>   of Clark and McClure in 1876.

In McGregor, at the School House Café
the waitress tells us to be sure to visit
the other buildings nearby. Three small cottages
cleverly filled with a mix of antiques and gift market finds
located on the edge of the town, population 381,
on a two lane highway buzzing with cars
all going somewhere else.

It's astonishing that a business that relied on the retail trade
picked a location almost guaranteed to fail.
What's not so surprising is that someone chose to try.
These small Minnesota towns are like jewels waiting to be mined.
If it weren't for winter this state might have been invaded long ago
by the type of developer who made Florida the place
everyone from New York and New Jersey wants to live.

But for those who first discover the value
of this last remaining wilderness there is no happy ending.
They will be like the early loggers who remembered
the giant hardwood forests they helped to destroy.

Bells

The town's
new carillon
plays hundreds
of tunes perfectly
like a well-behaved
pupil, but I preferred
the uncertainty of the old bells
the way the wind took the sounds
to play with, bending
the notes like
a blues man.

Rural Score

Beneath the sagging canopy
of an abandoned gas station,

two dozen six foot hollyhocks
stand guard like weary sentries.

Chamomile tucked in cracked cement
releases sweet fragrance with each step

Across the highway, seagulls follow
furrows left by a tractor that turns the earth

leaving black lines, dotted with white birds,
a kind of sheet music for the lan

At the Café during WeFest

Today's special is a raspberry muffin,
the waitress tells me, made fresh
with berries from a local gardener.
She's the only one on duty. She takes orders,
refills coffee cups, clears tables of dirty dishes,
still has time to joke with the customers.

At the counter, men in seed caps
linger over coffee. A motorcycle rider,
bronzed hair and seal-slick skin,
takes a booth by the door.
She wears tight fitting pants
and a vest that smells like new leather.

The overhead fans move so slowly
that if you watch them long enough
they seem to reverse rotation.
I motion to the waitress for a refill,
she saunters over with a full pot,
not a drop spilled.

For a poet there's nothing better
than observing, cataloguing, admiring.
Maybe loving, but that's been tried
and left me breathless.

Along the Northern Pacific Route—Economic Lesson #1

Trains, one hundred freight cars long
travel through small Minnesota towns
fifty, sixty times a day carrying coal,
oil and west coast graffiti.

Hanjin containers bound for New York,
coal for the electric generation plants,
shiny tank cars filled with black gold
from the oil fields of North Dakota
where adventure beckons.

Some towns have banned train whistles,
but the wheels of the trains
on the cold metal tracks still whisper
Destiny to workers in the trackside
factories, grain elevators, feed mills.

In one town, a worker at the boatworks
stops his hammering and listens.
Destiny, Destiny, say the train cars
clicking over the rails, heavy with profits,
commanding respect.

Each night at 3 a.m. the passenger train arrives.
He imagines climbing aboard, his hand
grasping the cold metal rail as he mounts
the steps to the Pullman car.

Minutes later, the train begins its slow creep,
gathering momentum, wheels clacking.
Destiny! Destiny! Destiny!

Washington, D.C.—Economic Lesson #2

This city is a slow riser,
garbage collectors sound the first bell.
A homeless man repacks his bedroll,
emerges from the arches of the
old Post Office building.

Forty years ago I lived in New York City.
Some days on my way to work I'd see
an occasional bum sprawled on a park bench
but most stayed downtown on the Bowery
where they were quickly forgotten.

Today, in the nation's capital, homeless and
haute couture mingle on every block.
It's not so easy to forget
we are all one world.

Back home in Minnesota,
in a small town whose entrance sign proclaims
it refuses to participate in the economic downturn,
a man is being evicted from his house
for being unable to pay the rent.

Later that winter he walks into the park
evicts the blackbirds from the snowy branches
and hangs himself from a sturdy tree
where his body stays for several days, rent-free.

Winter Roulette

Not just the first icy patch
but the second, the third and so on
an accident on every one

a pick-up truck spun out of control
hits the rock-hard snow of late winter
flips on its back like a surprised turtle

shaken bodies emerge
wave away their would-be rescuers
next, a yellow sports car overturned
in the median between east and west lanes

men form a silent circle around the wreckage
a police officer leads a woman away
face cupped in her hands

impossible to tell which way they were heading
now the only direction is back
to home, to hospital or to dust

it's snowing again, by morning
the ditches will be unbroken white
ready for the next turn of the wheel.

February

Thin winter sun
pierces clenched nerves
leaves a hint
of warmth
before burying itself
mole-like
in the dark fabrics
that cloak the house
in winter.

Slow Melt

Beneath a fogged mirror sky
a great blue heron stands in black water
eyes with disfavor the dirty snow
clinging to river's edge.

Robins, recently arrived,
peck at patches of cold ground.
Leafless trees appear a little out of focus
with the fuzz of new growth.

Hungry for color, my eyes search
barren swamps for red dogwood
roadside ditches for blue Pasque flowers,
some way to love this vacant wasteland,
in the slow melt between winter and spring.

Fast Spring

Three days after the first
official day of spring
there are leaf buds on
the honeysuckle.

A robin races round and round
the new green grass
like a first grader
released from school.

Does he remember?
This time last year
the snow was toddler high,
the ground hard frozen
the mole, the beetle, fast asleep.

Some years in Minnesota
the ice is barely off the lakes in time
for the fishing opener, an unofficial holiday
that seems to coincide with Mother's Day.

This year it's 72 degrees before the first of May.
Grass is green, woods filled with white blossoms,
wild plums, juneberries, chokecherries,
signal that morels are ready to be found.

Parade

Over the lake
  the wind strides

               dragging
        his great purple cape

          rippling the water

        At shore's edge
  grasses bow in homage

  trees in the forest
wave and wave

and wave.

Tornado

After the June rains, we returned
to the tumbled town and heard
the story a hundred times that day
on the news, in the café.

In some neighborhoods
the damage seems random
a roof here, a wall there,
a whole garage uprooted,
replanted a block away.

In the countryside, they say
cows hang in trees with pieces
of tin from metal buildings
that looked like kites
sailing on an unholy wind.

Here at the center there is nothing
undamaged, unturned, unskewed.
Trees uprooted, cemetery stones
tossed about like children's blocks.

No lives were lost, thank God,
though one man's heart gave out later
as he surveyed the broken town.
Like war, everyone dies a little bit.
No one talks about it anymore.

One Perfect Summer Evening

A brass septet plays a concert
on the shores of Spirit Lake, near Menahga,
a town named for the blueberry
that grows wild in the woods,

food for bears, Native Americans
and later, the Finns, who settled the area
because it reminded them of their homeland.
Rocks for the sauna, wood for warmth
water for the soul.

The brass players are Finns,
known for both melancholy and musicianship.
Tonight they play Finnish melodies
and popular American tunes
as elegantly as a chamber orchestra.

Trees on the shoreline catch the notes,
sift through them, tasting immortality.
On the giant drum of the lake
waves beat cadences of their own.

Late Summer

It's late August but because there's been so much rain the trees and grass are still unseasonably green.

The crabapple litters the lawn with bright red fruit, attracting bees and a pair of doves. High cirrus,

heralds of winter, replace the puffy cumulus of summer. Now and then a wispy cloud scurries across the sky,

a straggler swan hurrying to join the flock.

Signs of Fall

Except for the bales of hay
the corn tall and tasseled
it might be summer's start
and not its end.

In the green woods, the poplar leaves
have turned to yellow and gold
like anxious debutantes
trying on dresses
for the Harvest Ball.

Home Again

The old house smells familiar.
On the news a circus performer
has fallen fifty feet to her death.

The weeds rioted while I was gone,
the blossoms of the tree lilac
exploded like 4th of July rockets.

That was expected. What I didn't expect
was how the lake would follow me home.

The air today is perfect,
still and heavy with dew.
Except for the news and the weeds
I might still be on vacation.

I have carried some of the lake
home with me. If I'm careful
I won't spill it.

Poet, historian and musician **Lina Belar** has written about giant pumpkins, century farms, teenage suicide, veterans' stories and the arts, far ranging topics that collectively define rural Minnesota.

Her poetry has been featured in *Talking Stick, Lake Region Review*, and Northern Lights Library Network's *Poets Across Minnesota*. Her narrative writing includes press releases, radio news, articles for trade magazines, and grants for historic preservation, digitization, and veterans' stories.A resident of Minnesota since 1974, she writes regular newspaper columns in which she displays her genuine affection for local history.

In her spare time she plays keyboard for two area churches and trumpet with Heartland Symphony Orchestra and Long Prairie Chamber Orchestra.

www.ingramcontent.com/pod-product-compliance
Lightning Source LLC
LaVergne TN
LVHW041524070426
835507LV00012B/1799